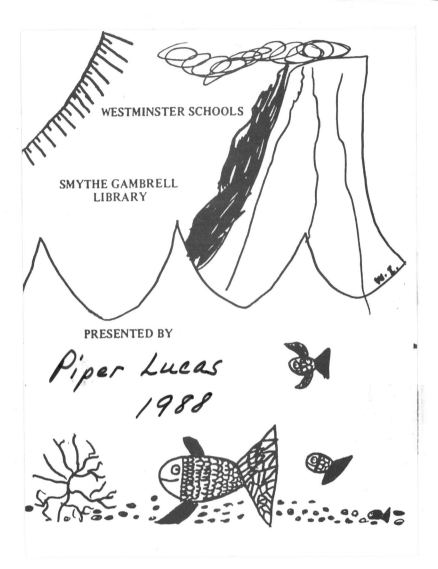

WESTMINSTER SCHOOLS

SMYTHE GAMBRELL
LIBRARY

PRESENTED BY

Piper Lucas
1988

CASTLES

RICHARD CLARK

The Bookwright Press
New York · 1986

Topics

The Age of the Dinosaurs
Castles
Earthquakes and Volcanoes
Great Disasters
Houses and Homes
Peoples of the World
Pollution and Conservation
Robots
Under the Ground

All the words that appear
in **bold** are explained in the
glossary on page 30.

First published in the
United States in 1986 by
The Bookwright Press
387 Park Avenue South
New York, NY 10016

First published in 1985 by
Wayland (Publishers) Ltd
61 Western Road, Hove
East Sussex BN3 1JD, England

© Copyright 1985 Wayland (Publishers) Ltd

ISBN 0–531–18057–3
Library of Congress Catalog Card Number: 85–73661

Phototypeset by Kalligraphics Ltd
Redhill, Surrey, England
Printed in Italy by
G. Canale & C.S.p.A., Turin

Contents

Castles Around the World

The castles that you read about in story-books, like King Arthur's Camelot, usually sound like pretty and romantic places. The real ones were not. They were built by emperors, kings, princes and noblemen to protect themselves from local bandits, invading armies and even sometimes from their own people.

They were either large fortresses or **fortified** homes, built to protect the owner, his family and possessions. A castle would either stand alone, in a place which could easily be defended, or it would be part of a fortified city, like the Palace of the Popes in Avignon, France.

Peñafiel, Spain, was built on a hill for protection.

The ruins of Great Zimbabwe.

Throughout history, all peoples and civilizations have built castles. About 1,500 years ago, in Yucatan, Mexico, the Mayan people built the great walled city of Chichen-Itza using giant stone slabs fitted together without cement.

In biblical times, King Herod built Masada on a hilltop in what is now Israel. Here a group of 960 Jews held out against a Roman army for two years, and then committed suicide rather than give in to the Romans. In southern Africa, you can still see the ruins of Great Zimbabwe, built about 800 years ago by the Shona people.

The Red Fort at Delhi.

In India, in the seventeenth century, the conquering Moguls from Persia built the impressive Red Fort at Delhi. Their **allies**, the Rajputs, built castles like the awesome Amber Palace, which sits on a hillside overlooking Jaipur city.

Forts are not usually homes for royalty, but, like castles, they are self-contained and built to withstand attack or siege. When early settlers in the American West needed protection from angry Indian tribes, they built log forts such as Fort Laramie in Wyoming. Another famous fort was the Alamo, in Texas, where Davy Crockett and Jim Bowie died fighting the Mexican army in 1836.

The Romans built many stone forts to station troops throughout their vast empire. A familiar type of castle in western Europe is the kind the Normans adapted from these Roman forts. The Norman castle at Dover, England, and the

In the United States, log forts were built to protect traders and settlers from Indian tribes.

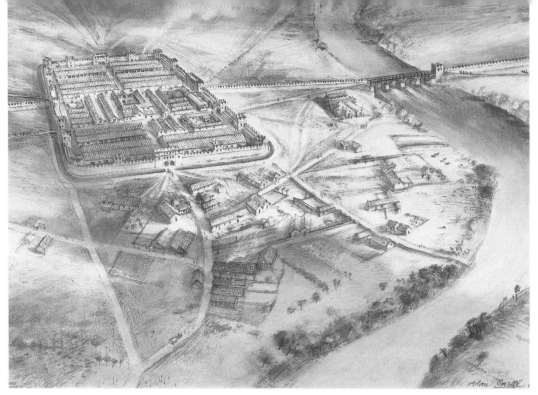

The Romans built many forts like this to station their troops throughout their vast empire.

Tower of London were both built on the sites of old Roman forts.

In the Middle Ages, the **Crusaders** brought back ideas about castle-building from the Holy Land and Constantinople (modern Istanbul). In Lebanon today are the remains of Krak des Chevaliers, the most famous castle built by the Crusader knights to terrify their Saracen enemies.

In Wales, Edward I of England built a great chain of castles including Harlech, Conwy and Caernarfon, to keep down the rebellious Welsh and their leaders, Prince Llewellyn and Owen Glendower.

In France whole cities, such as Carcassonne and Orange, were fortified against wandering bands of ex-soldiers who terrorized the countryside between wars. Germany has a string of castles along the Rhine River and other important rivers. In fact, there are still remains of the castles of the past in most countries of the world.

The impressive city walls at Carcassonne, France.

How Castles were Built

The first castles were made of great rings of stone and earth surrounded by ditches. These were topped by strong log fences, with gates that could be easily defended. In wartime, farmers would bring their families and animals into the safety of the "castle," where there would be water wells and pits to store food in. Maiden Castle, in Dorset, England, is an example. It was used for 2,000 years before it was captured by the Romans in the first century AD.

Maiden Castle was used for over 2,000 years.

When the Normans, led by William the Conqueror, invaded Saxon England in 1066 they quickly began building simple castles throughout the country to protect themselves in their new kingdom. First, the local peasants were forced to build a great mound of earth, called a "motte," and then a square wooden tower (or "keep") was built on top of it. The area below the great mound was surrounded by a high wooden fence. This was called the "bailey."

In times of war, farmers and their families sought safety within the castle's defenses.

A Norman motte-and-bailey castle.

Castle Acre, in Norfolk, England, is a motte-and-bailey type of castle.

Eventually, the wooden buildings and fences of these motte-and-bailey castles were replaced by stone towers and walls. Early earth-and-timber castles were built in a few weeks, but the larger stone castles sometimes took many years to construct and needed many more workers. It took nearly 2,000 laborers to build Caernarfon Castle, in Wales. The stone walls had deep **foundations**, and while the lower parts were solid, the upper parts had passages and little rooms in them, where servants and soldiers lived. There were also small slits where archers could fire arrows down at enemies below.

The entrance to a castle was its weakest point, so a strong gatehouse, called a "barbican," was built to protect it. The barbican contained a **drawbridge** to span the **moat**, and perhaps a **portcullis** as well.

At the center of the castle would be the huge keep where weapons and armor were stored, and where people often lived. In many castles the **great hall** and the living quarters of the lord and his family would be in the keep. In other castles, these rooms would be built alongside the walls. Typical **medieval** castles are Bodiam in Sussex, England, Beaumaris on the

It took 2,000 laborers to build the castle at Caernarfon, in Wales.

Isle of Anglesey (a county of Wales) and Tarascon in Provence, France.

There would be a parade ground in front of the keep where soldiers practiced and young **squires** learned to handle horses, swords and lances. It was also here that knights **jousted** with blunted **lances**, or if they had a serious quarrel, decided who was guilty and who was innocent with a fierce battle to the death.

Bodiam, in Sussex, England, is a good example of a medieval castle.

Life in a Castle

Castles were busy and lively places, but the first thing you would notice if you went back in time to a castle in the fourteenth century would probably be the smell! Farmyard animals and the war horses of the lord and his knights would live in stables around the great courtyard, or even roam free.

The great hall, where the lord and his lady held banquets for important visitors, would be full of dogs, and plenty of cats to catch the rats. The walls of the great hall might be covered with plaster and painted, or draped with large woven tapestries. The floors were of stone or wood, with dry reeds to

A medieval banquet scene.

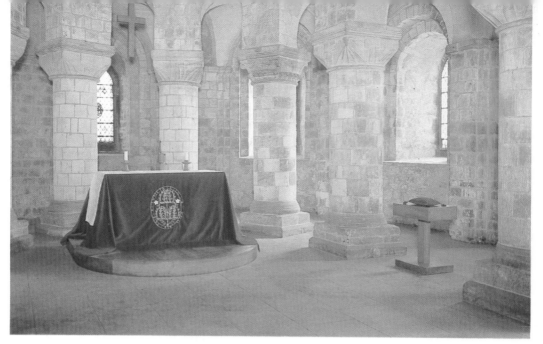

Religion was an important part of medieval life, and every castle had its own chapel.

cover them. They were rarely cleaned, and the reeds were left until they rotted. The windows had wooden shutters because glass was very expensive. The whole building would be hot and smelly in summer, and damp and cold in winter.

All the rubbish was thrown into a stinking open pit called a "midden." There were no bathrooms, even in the grandest castles; toilets were just holes that emptied into the moat. They were located in tiny rooms that stuck out from the walls. People rarely bathed, except perhaps once a year.

People found simple ways of having fun. The lord of the castle always had his own **jester**, and there

Cooking was done in large kitchens.

were singing minstrels who went from castle to castle entertaining people and giving them the latest news. There were often fairs on holy days, with acrobats, conjurers, jugglers and **peddlers**.

There was always lots of work to be done, because everything in the castle had to be made by local craftspeople. Even a small castle had saddlers, shoemakers, blacksmiths and armorers, as well as carpenters and stonemasons to repair the walls.

The larger castles would have bakers, butchers, candlemakers, tailors to make simple clothes, and weavers to provide the woolen cloth, all working in tiny workshops nearby. Inside the castle there might be dozens or even hundreds of servants, and a large number of cooks working in a vast kitchen. There would also be brewers and wine sellers (because everyone drank beer or wine instead of the foul water), dairy workers and many humble laborers.

How a medieval keep might have looked inside.

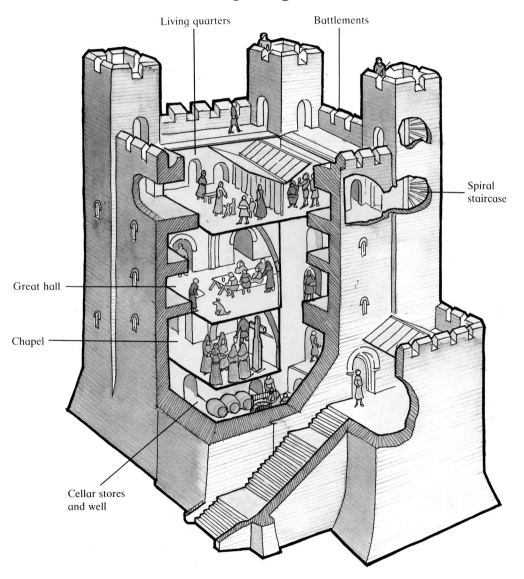

Living quarters

Battlements

Spiral staircase

Great hall

Chapel

Cellar stores and well

Attack and Defense

What made castles so important in ancient warfare was that an advancing enemy would not dare to pass a castle or walled city for fear of being attacked from behind. Castles defended river crossings, mountain passes and other important places.

There were several ways of capturing a castle: battering down the gates and walls, starving the people in the castle until they gave in, and **bribery** or **treachery**.

The simplest **siege** weapon was the battering ram, a huge log with a metal tip shaped like a ram's head. A team of men crashed the battering ram against the castle gates until the gates gave way. This was dangerous, because the defenders shot at them with

Norman soldiers fire a stone-throwing catapult.

longbows, crossbows, big mechanical javelin-throwers and even small cannon. From the safety of the castle **battlements** they dropped stones and poured boiling liquid or a burning substance called "Greek Fire" on the soldiers below. Greek Fire could burn the attackers alive inside their suits of armor or chain mail.

Tall ladders were used to try and climb over the castle walls. In addition, tall wooden towers were built and propped up against the walls. These gave protection to the soldiers who climbed up ladders inside the towers and then rushed across the battlements to attack the defenders.

Sometimes miners (called "sappers") tunneled under the walls and then set fire to the wooden props

Crusader soldiers are attacked with Greek Fire.

that held up the earth above the tunnel. When the wooden props burned away, the tunnel and the wall above it collapsed. A deep moat around a castle would keep sappers from tunneling.

Château Gaillard, in France, was originally built by Richard the Lionheart, King of England. It was captured in 1204 when King John's English forces were besieged by the armies of Philip II of France. The French sappers cracked one of the walls, and

A fierce battle before a walled city.

then pounded the weak spot with huge stone-throwing catapults until part of it fell down.

If these siege weapons did not work, the besiegers could try to starve the defenders out. This was often the most successful way of defeating a castle, but it took a long time.

In fact, castles were rarely captured quickly. In 1266, Kenilworth Castle in England held out for six months before being taken by its attackers. Even more impressive was the city of Carthage, on the Mediterranean coast. It was besieged by the

Carthage was besieged by Rome for three years.

The remains of Corfe Castle, in Dorset, England.

Romans for three years until it fell in 146 BC.

Sometimes the attackers had to hope that one of the defenders would betray the others and show them a way into the castle, or they might try to bribe someone to let them in. Corfe Castle, in Dorset, fell to Oliver Cromwell's army during the English Civil War through treachery alone. Sometimes the soldiers inside a castle turned against the lord who had hired them to defend him.

Things changed when the attackers began to use powerful cannon. Few stone walls could stand up to the fire of large siege cannon for long. After about AD 1400, castles became less important in warfare. They were still built as fortified houses, but rarely as large fortresses.

Royal Castles

The biggest and most impressive castles were usually built by **monarchs**. For instance, the Tower of London was first a royal home and only later did it become a prison and a place of execution. Today it is a museum where you can still see many of the weapons used in ancient warfare, and where the Crown Jewels of England are kept.

Unlike the Tower of London, Windsor Castle in Berkshire is still used as a home by Queen Elizabeth II. Her other homes, such as Balmoral in Scotland and Sandringham in the east of England, are not true castles because they are not fortified.

Windsor Castle is still used as a royal home.

No one was supposed to build a castle without the permission of the reigning king or queen, but the more powerful noblemen sometimes went ahead with it even if permission was refused. In England, important families such as the Percys of Alnwick, in Northumberland, and the Dukes of Norfolk (who built Arundel Castle in Sussex) were almost as powerful as their kings. The same was true in France

The Alcazar at Segovia, Spain, is one of Europe's many royal castles.

Glamis castle, Scotland.

and other European countries.

Castles could sometimes become prisons for kings and queens. In 1327 Edward II of England was tortured to death at Berkeley Castle in

Gloucestershire, and in 1400 Richard II was murdered at Pontefract Castle in Yorkshire. Fotheringay Castle in Northamptonshire, where Mary Queen of Scots was executed in 1587, is now just a mound of earth.

There are many royal castles throughout Europe, such as Castel Nuovo in Italy, which was the home of the King of Naples for many years. The soaring Alcazar of Segovia, in Spain, once the home of the kings of Castile, rises up dramatically from a rocky crag. The royal castles of Elsinore in Denmark, and Glamis in Scotland, were made famous through the plays *Hamlet* and *Macbeth*, by William

The Kremlin was the home of the Russian Tsars.

Shakespeare. The Kremlin, in Moscow, was the headquarters of the Russian Tsars until the seventeenth century.

"Mad" King Ludwig II of Bavaria (which is now part of West Germany) built a series of beautiful castles in the nineteenth century. The greatest of them all is Neuschwanstein (see front cover).

Modern royal families do not build castles any more, but wealthy people were still building fake castles earlier this century. Castle Drogo, a **stately home** in Devon, England was finished in 1930. An

Castle Drogo, Devon, England, completed in 1930.

San Simeon has its own swimming pool.

even more famous fake castle, called San Simeon, was built in the 1920s by the newspaper millionaire William Randolph Hearst, in California. San Simeon was put together using bits and pieces from hundreds of old buildings all over Europe.

Today, castles are still exciting places to wander around and investigate. If you take a trip abroad, you can visit some ancient castles to find out how people lived hundreds of years ago.

Glossary

Allies Friendly countries or states, which join together for a common purpose.

Battlements Walls on a building with openings from which to fire arrows or guns.

Bribery Giving a secret gift to persuade someone to do something dishonest or illegal.

Crusader Someone who fought for the Christian armies to recapture the Holy Land from the Moslem Saracens in the Middle Ages.

Drawbridge A bridge that can be drawn up or let down.

Fortified Strengthened against attack.

Foundations The base of building below ground.

Great hall The main living room of a medieval house or castle.

Jester A clown, employed at the court of a king or nobleman, to amuse his master and his master's guests.

Joust A sporting combat between two mounted knights with lances.

Lance A long spear.

Medieval To do with the period in history known as the Middle Ages (roughly AD1000–1500).

Moat A deep trench around a castle, often full of water.

Monarch A king, queen, emperor or empress.

Peddler Someone who travels around with goods for sale.

Portcullis A large grating that can be let down quickly to close a gateway.

Siege An attempt to capture a castle, town or city by surrounding it so that no help can reach it.

Squire A boy who served a knight in preparation for becoming a knight himself.

Stately home In England, a very large, luxurious house.

Treachery The act of betraying people who trust you; an act of disloyalty or treason.

Books to Read

Davison, Brian. *Explore a Castle.* North Pomfret, VT: David & Charles, 1983.

Gee, Robyn, ed. *Living in Castle Times: First Book of History.* Tulsa, OK: E D C Publishing, 1982.

Macauley, David. *Castle.* Boston: Houghton Mifflin, 1977.

Miquel, Pierre. *Castles of the Middle Ages.* Morristown, NJ: Silver Burdett, 1985.

Odor, Ruth S. *Learning about Castles and Palaces.* Chicago: Childrens Press, 1982.

Sancha, Sheila. *The Castle Story.* New York: Thomas Y. Crowell, Junior Books, 1982.

Spellman, Linda. *Castles, Codes, and Calligraphy.* Santa Barbara: Learning Works, 1984.

Picture Acknowledgments

AA Photo Library 23; John Avon 18; British Tourist Authority 13, 24; Camerapix Hutchison Library (Timothy Beddow) 4, (Simon McBride) 5, (Bernard Gerard) 26, (John Griffiths-Jones) 27, (Bernard Regent) 29; Eric Crichton/Bruce Coleman Ltd 14; Department of the Environment 8, 10, 16, 17; Museum of London 11; National Trust 28; Topham Picture Library 9; Wayland Picture Library 15, 21, 25; Peter Newark's Western Americana 7; Gerry Wood 12, 19, 20, 22; ZEFA 6.

Index

10.09